Secrets of Cloud Computing

Terms and Conditions

LEGAL NOTICE

The Publisher has strived to be as accurate and complete as possible in the creation of this report, notwithstanding the fact that he does not warrant or represent at any time that the contents within are accurate due to the rapidly changing nature of the Internet.

While all attempts have been made to verify information provided in this publication, the Publisher assumes no responsibility for errors, omissions, or contrary interpretation of the subject matter herein. Any perceived slights of specific persons, peoples, or organizations are unintentional.

In practical advice books, like anything else in life, there are no guarantees of income made. Readers are cautioned to reply on their own judgment about their individual circumstances to act accordingly.

This book is not intended for use as a source of legal, business, accounting or financial advice. All readers are advised to seek services of competent professionals in legal, business, accounting and finance fields.

You are encouraged to print this book for easy reading.

Table Of Contents

Foreword

Cloud computing is basically the term used to describe anything involving the delivering processes hosted services over the internet. These services are generally divided into three main categories, which would be infrastructure as a service, platform as a service and software as a service. The depiction of the cloud symbol is probably why the process is called as such. Get all the info you need here.

Cloud Computing Secrets

Chapter 1:

Synopsis

Cloud services are distinct in its makeup and are certainly different from the more tradition al hosting process. With the cloud service there is the leeway to sell on demand, which is usually by the minute or hour, it is also elastic which means a user can dictate the amount of service needed at any given time and the service is fully managed by the provider.

This would effectively mean the customer would need nothing else but a personal computer and access to the internet. Some of the reasons cloud has become so popular is because this element is able to provide significant innovations in virtualization and distributed computing, while improving access to high speed internet.

The Basics

Configured to be either private of public the cloud is able to switch comfortably between the two while still providing the necessary services on both sides.

The public cloud sell services to anyone on the internet while the private cloud functions more as a proprietary network or data centre that supplies hosted services to a limited group. However the end goal of the cloud would be to provide easy, scalable access to computing resources and IT services.

The infrastructure as a service allow a company to pay for only the capacity needed and to only buy online as required. The platform as a service is defined as a set of software and product development tool that is hosted on the provider's infrastructure.

The software as a service is where the vendor supplies the hardware infrastructure, the software product and interacts with the user through a front end portal.

Chapter 2:

Synopsis

The rather delicate process of conveying and using information technology services and resources is the basics providing element of the cloud computing. For some cloud computing is a paradigm where information is permanently stored in servers on the internet and cached temporarily on clients that include tools for such online purposes.

The Benefits

Perhaps the first thing that should be noted is the fact that the cloud computing models are not owned by the users but are instead rented or paid for when needed. Although this may seem like loss of control, the other points far outdo this thought process.

 The most compelling attraction would be the lower costs involved in utilizing the cloud tool, as this will help the companies to focus on their goods and services rather than having to come with funds to constantly upgrade their computer systems.

The lowering of the technology based capital in no way effects the access to devices and locations independently, thus enabling the user access to systems anywhere and anytime.

There is also better overall performance, load balancing and even locating data processes with much lower overall costs involved when comparisons are made with the older and more conventional methods previously used.

Cloud computing is also reputed to be able to contribute to a higher affect of reliability and scalability in many positive ways, one of which is in the area of data security. The security improves considerably although some data may be lost as the system automatically seems to eliminate these.

Cloud computing also is able to produce better and more improved resource utilization where there is sustainability in movement such as green technology or clean technology. Most of the bigger companies are taking an active role in this seemingly new addition to the equation of providing better service possibilities.

Chapter 3:

Is Cloud Computing Really Secured?

Synopsis

A growing number of users are turning to the use of cloud computing, but the question remains on its security levels. There is no doubt that cloud computing has been able to change the way most users manage their networks. Although this is attractive as its obvious contributions to the cost cutting exercise, there is still the question of security as the information is shared across multiple servers.

Have A Look

For the most part, those in the industry would agree that cloud computing is relatively secure by comparison. The security levels by comparison are not really any different from the standard computing and hosting platforms used. Commonly thought of as disastrous, outages are the concerns of most users who tend to go into a panic when the bigger players like Google suffer this.

However it should be understood that these outages are relatively common and are bound to occur periodically, thus the users should be comforted with the fact that this does not necessarily mean information is lost or hacked.

This in turn makes the users more aware of the security issues and causes them to take more care in tightening their policies and physical security measures. Most users will not consistently monitor their networks and take action as soon as any intrusion is detected. This may include step to ensure the data received is encrypted to ensure those who are not supposed to be privy to the information will not be able to read it, and most traditional hosts will offer the relevant back up after each transaction is made almost instantly.

Users may also encrypt their own information before it is submitted to further heighten the security measures already in place. Therefore it is fast becoming an undisputed fact that cloud computing is fast gaining mileage in the online arena.

Chapter 4:

What Is Public Cloud All About?

Synopsis

As its title depicts, public cloud computing is based on the standard cloud computing model, where a service provider makes resources, such as applications and storage available to anyone and everyone over the internet. Most of these are free or offered on a pay per use format.

Public Cloud

There are several benefits to this type of service or system and that is why it is fast making inroads on the internet platform. The most innovative system to date that is able to provide essentials in an easy and inexpensive set up, is simply attributed to the hardware, application and bandwidth costs which are all covered by the provider.

The scalability issues are also adequately addressed and at mostly adequately met to the end users satisfaction. There is also very little or no wastage of resources as the user would only pay for what is being used or due to the fact that some of the elements come free of any costs.

Basically the actual term of public cloud was first used to differentiate between the standard model and the private cloud which is both commonly used. This is a proprietary network or data center that uses cloud computing technologies such as virtualization. The private could is managed but the organization it serves and a portion of the model, the hybrid cloud, is maintained by both internal and external providers.

Having a delivery system that does all computing and storage actions as a service to the end recipient is definitely an advantage to all users. These services are entrusted to the user's data, software and computations over a secure network. The end user could ideally access the cloud based on applications through a web browser or a light weight desktop or mobile application while the business software and date are stored on the servers at even remote locations. .

Chapter 5:

Understanding The Concept of Private Cloud

Synopsis

The point of the private cloud concept would be that it allows any company or individual user to create its own database center with the execution of just a few clicks. The whole exercise would only require a few minutes and the platform created would be fully operational and ready to accommodate the user's needs.

The private cloud system will be based on components within the infrastructure that are dedicated exclusively to one client for any purpose which would include storage and network facilities. These elements are always accessible and designed to provide 100% network availability to each user. The resources provided will usually be backed in a way that ideally prevents any failures where each element instituting the host and storage are redundant, thus having the dual power, dual mains input, and dual inventor, dual switch and any others that would require the dual concept..

Private

The single interface system will manage the entire infrastructure of the private cloud and this has certainly won the confidence of its users. The recognizable fact of the reliability allows customers to instantly carry out all their needs, which may include add a server, crate a virtual machine, and take advantage of storage and others.

Whatever the need, the user simply has to select the desired hardware directly from the client interface and it becomes immediately available and ready for use.

This is of course a huge advantage as there is no longer a need to spend huge amount of time and resources getting the infrastructure done from basics.

This in turn allows all those involved to have access to all the tools to implement the ideas and doesn't restrict any controlling, connecting and configuration of features. At the same time all this is kept private and only privy to the intended parties.

Chapter 6:

Hybrid Cloud and It's Advantages

Synopsis

As the hybrid cloud gains momentum in the industry, there are a lot of interesting and advantages issues that are the contributing factors to its popularity. This is of course very important to the end user who is constantly looking for ways to enhance the online experience.

Great Info

More businesses are making the transition to the cloud platform of which hybrid seems to take on the bigger share of interests. Its impact on being able to provide creating, processing, sharing and disposal of data is all part of the attraction, as many users are becoming more aware of the benefits of blending the in house and outsources computing and networking resources, thus the preparation to suit the hybrid model in on the rise.

Most cloud users would justify the hybrid cloud as being able to offer greater flexibility to meet the changing data needs that are constantly evolving to provide the user with the best options.

The hybrid cloud is also designed to accommodate movements of applications easily between public and private as needed and back again.

Being able to select the data that remains within the private cloud and that which is to be made available on the public cloud platform is something that the hybrid cloud is capable of creating.

The ability of being able to use multiple clouds for different applications and to be able to allocate different elements of a particular application to external and internal environments can also be done with the hybrid cloud.

Using the hybrid will allow the user to create an approach to the architecture, as considerations for mixing and matching resources between local infrastructure and with infrastructure that is scalable and provisioned on demand. By placing the applications and data on the best platforms the user will be able to span the processing between the two.

Chapter 7:

Synopsis

The features of cloud computing which contributes to a more efficient and opportune way of creating revenue and newer channels for business without the added cost makes it a very viable platform to explore.

Understanding the various different cloud computing systems will allow the user to make an informed choice as to the suitability of a particular cloud for the business intended. Therefore in the quest to gain this understanding, the user should take note of the following depictions as it could prove to be useful in the eventual choices made.

There are basically 5 different types of clouds currently being used, designed or in the making. The proprietary platform of cloud that provide various services would include Google (type 1), Microsoft (type 2), and other large IT players (type 3), which would include the likes of IBM, Apple, HP and Amazon.

For Your Business

There are also the additions of the service type cloud (type 4) where many cloud service providers offer a variety of services. These could range from web and applications hosting clouds to vertical industry clouds. Players such as Telcos, web hosts, ISVs SaaS are all part of the type 4 platform providers.

Last but not in any the least would be the clouds that are run by enterprise IT (type 5) where services provided will be for internal use and by employees and partners. The in house clouds of large companies would make up the bulk of those making this choice.

The competitive nature of the business environment requires the advantage provided for by using the type 5 or the outsourcing of the type 4 clouds.

This need is met through the creation of solutions, ecosystems and partnerships with service providers and businesses to build and operate efficient service clouds.

Chapter 8:

Key Features of Cloud Computing

Synopsis

It is important to be able to identify if the applications offered are really cloud computing compatible as there are some that simply have the labels depicting such features without actually being able to do so.

Basically the cloud computing application allows businesses to increase IT capacity or adds on capabilities for the user anytime and anywhere. This is done without the requirement of immediate costs for new infrastructure, training new personnel on licensing new software or can also be used as a pay per use service.

Features

The following are some of the identifiable features of cloud computing that should be present in the applications chosen:

The on demand self service is an attractive feature that is commonly sought after by many users for its obvious contributory factors. Here the users are able to set themselves up without the need to have the assistance of others not the need to pay for such assistance to be rendered.

Ubiquitous network access which is available though the standard internet using the relevant enable devices of choice of the user. This is very useful as the devices need to be streamlined in nature to accommodate the needs of the moment.

Location independent resource pooling will contribute to the easy processing and storage demands that are balanced across a common infrastructure with no particular resource being assigned to any user at any given time. The rapid elasticity also creates the platform for the users, to increase or decrease the capacity as and when they choose to do so.

Pay per use is also another feature that is popular and trumped only by the possible free feature. The user can be charges according to the fees based on the usage of a combination of computing power, bandwidth use and storage.

Chapter 9:

Revolutionize Your Business With Cloud Computing

Synopsis

The constant advancement of technology is often the driving force behind the IT industry's push to make newer discoveries and inventions available to the general user. This demand on the part of the user will create the necessity to have better applications and tools to enhance even the business side of the user's requirements.

As technology has advance even further, so has the emergence of the cloud computing has been able to revolutionize the workings of business worldwide. Generally cloud computing is an application that facilitates the storage of data, processes information and retains setting on a central server as needed.

This in turn allow the critical data to be stored and retrieved anytime and anywhere is a safe functioning platform which help to prevent the accidental loss of data through other external disturbances.

For Your Business

The cloud computing is able to help the user of the internet to transfer files and data according to the needs of the business endeavor undertaken. Some cloud computing allows the user to store and backup financial software on a central server whole other may require it to do other exercise for the business as a whole.

This is done in a quick and efficient manner which is much better than the more complex and previously conventional way of getting such tasks done.

The cloud computing benefits the user in terms of broadband internet connections where a user may be interested in transmitting high definition images and audio information in real time.

This is a great way for users to stream movies, audio files and other information with comparatively phenomenal speeds. There is also the facility of being able to store of back up all the files and folders on a central serves to he used by other privy to the information too..

Wrapping Up

Like any other assisting tool to be used for creating easy and flexible usage, the cloud computing provider has to be carefully chosen to ensure the fit is compatible with the requirement of the user.

Once the decision has been made to actually use a cloud, the user should ideally then explore the various options available before setting on a cloud computing system that is most suited to the needs intended. Part of the exercise should be to ensure the cloud computing service provider is able to provide reliability and viability on any of the more complex areas it is managing.

The following are some of the elements to be aware of when choosing the right cloud computing provider:

- Service level agreements and monitoring requirements - for the user buying the service from the cloud service provider there should ideally be a acceptable standard that is workable for both parties. There should always be some leeway for negotiations as the user would ideally be entrusting to commit systems with probable sensitive information to the provider.

- The choice made should also include the commitment and support elements the cloud computing provide is able to extend to the user. It is important to ensure the support if forthcoming which the application s or infrastructures move to the chosen cloud. This will help the user to align its internal support team to deal with any elements either from the internal user of the cloud provider itself.

- Billing and accounting – this benefits the user as the payments are based on usage thus effectively creating the billing and account management that is ideally automated to ensure the user can monitor the usage and its costs incurred. This is especially useful for the cost conscious user.

www.ingramcontent.com/pod-product-compliance
Lightning Source LLC
LaVergne TN
LVHW050305200726
843509LV00015B/3162